VEGETARIAN COOKING
FOR BEGINNERS

Fiona Watt

Designed by Mary Cartwright
Illustrated by Kim Lane
Photography by Howard Allman
Recipes by Catherine Atkinson
American editor: Peggy Porter Tierney

Food preparation by Ricky Turner and Lizzie Harris
Cover illustration by Christyan Fox

Contents

Before you begin

All the recipes in this book are vegetarian, which means that they contain no meat or fish. Some of the recipes are suitable for 'vegans' or 'strict vegetarians'. These recipes don't use any animal products, such as cheese or eggs. They are marked with a (V) in the index (see page 48).

Before you start to cook any of the recipes in this book, read through the hints and tips on these two pages and page 4.

Ingredients

At the beginning of each recipe there is a list of ingredients. Make sure that you have them all before you start to cook. If you can't find some of the ingredients in your supermarket, look in your local health food store.

Preparing vegetables

You should wash all fresh vegetables before you prepare them. If you are using mushrooms, wipe them on a damp paper towel before slicing them.

Leeks need to be washed very well to get rid of any soil. See step 1, page 26.

The sections at the top of cauliflowe or broccoli are called florets. Cut these off the thick stalk (see page 2

A clove of garlic is one part of a whole garlic bulb. Peel it before you use it.

Use kitchen scissors to cut up fresh herbs, such as parsley or chives.

Peel carrots and potatoes if they are dirty or big. Wash or scrape new potatoes and small carrots.

Measuring with a cup or spoon

If you use a cup or spoon for measuring, make sure that the ingredient is level with the edge and not heaped up.

Getting your oven ready

The dishes in this book should be cooked on the middle shelf of an oven, unless the recipe says something else. Always move the shelf to the right place before you turn on your oven. If you have a fan oven, read its instruction book before you start to cook. It will tell you to reduce the heat or the cooking time.

A balanced diet

Your body needs proteins, vitamins and iron to stay healthy. If you eat a vegetarian diet all the time, it's important that your food contains a good mixture of them.

Iron can be found in things such as eggs, nuts and dried fruit.

Beans, nuts, eggs, cheese and milk all contain protein.

Cheese, milk, yogurt and eggs all contain essential vitamins. They are also found in many breakfast cereals and soya milk.

Hints and tips

This page shows you some of the cooking skills which are used in the recipes in this book.

Grating cheese

Cut a piece of cheese which is a little bigger than what you need, so that you do not need to grate all the way down to your fingers.

Adding salt and pepper

Try adding a pinch of salt or ground black pepper.

Some recipes tell you to add a little salt and pepper. The amount you add of each depends on your own taste.

Cutting peppers

Use a serrated knife to cut both ends off. Cut the pepper in half from end to end and cut out the part with the seeds.

If you are going to slice the pepper, it's a lot easier to cut from the inside, rather than trying to cut into the shiny skin.

Slicing tomatoes

A small serrated knife is best to use to slice a tomato. Cut the tomato in half, then lay it flat-side down and slice it.

Making breadcrumbs

1. For homemade breadcrumbs, get some two- or three-day-old bread. Cut off the crusts and tear the slices of bread into pieces.

2. Put the bread into a food processor. Put on the lid and turn it on. Whizz the bread until you get fine crumbs.

Use the small or medium holes on your grater.

If you don't have a food processor, grate stale bread on a cheese grater to make crumbs. Be careful that you don't grate your fingers.

Cheese crunchies

Makes 10-12

2oz. (¾ cup) grated mature Cheddar cheese
½ cup soft 'tub' margarine
½ cup semolina
½ cup self-rising flour
½ cup plain whole-wheat flour
quarter of a teaspoon of salt

1. Grate the cheese on the medium holes on your grater. Put the cheese into a large bowl. Add the margarine and semolina.

2. Shake the flour and the salt through a strainer into the bowl. Add any pieces left in the bottom of the strainer.

Use a wooden spoon.

3. Stir everything well until all the ingredients are mixed together. Then, squeeze the mixture into a ball.

4. Sprinkle a clean, dry work surface with a little flour. Put the mixture onto it and shape it into a roll, about 6in. long.

5. Lay the roll on some plastic foodwrap. Wrap it around the roll. Put the roll into a refrigerator for about an hour, to chill.

The margarine greases the baking sheets.

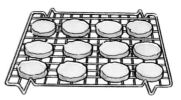

6. While the roll is in the refrigerator, dip a paper towel in some margarine, then rub it over two baking sheets.

7. Turn on your oven to 375°F. Unwrap the roll and cut it into ½in. slices. Space out the slices on the baking sheets.

8. Bake them for about 15 minutes until they are golden. When they are cooked, lift them onto a wire rack to cool.

Three-bean dip

Enough for 4-6

14oz. can of navy beans
14oz. can of pinto beans
14oz. can of cannellini beans
2 lemons
1 clove of garlic
5 tablespoons of tahini paste
4 tablespoons of boiling water
2 tablespoons of chopped parsley
salt and ground black pepper

1. Empty the beans into a strainer or colander. Rinse the beans under cold water, then drain them. Pour them into a large bowl.

Serve the dip with homemade breadsticks (see opposite), or with crackers.

Stir the beans too, to lift those at the bottom.

2. Mash the beans with a fork to make a smoothish mixture. It's quite hard work to begin with. Put some water on to boil.

3. Cut the lemons in half. Press and twist each half on a lemon squeezer. Pour the juice into the beans and mash the mixture again.

To serve, spoon the dip into a clean bowl and sprinkle on some more parsley.

4. Peel the garlic clove and crush it. Add the garlic to the beans along with the tahini, boiling water and the parsley.

5. Stir in a little salt and pepper. Then, beat the mixture with a wooden spoon until everything is mixed in thoroughly.

6. Taste it and add more salt and pepper if you need to. Put the dip into a refrigerator for at least half an hour to chill.

Breadsticks

Makes about 20

10oz. package of white bread machine mix
2 tablespoon of poppy seeds
2 tablespoons of sesame seeds
flour for work surface
margarine for greasing
yeast, if bread mix calls for it

Heat your oven to 400°F.

1. Grease two baking sheets with margarine on a paper towel. Open the bread mix and put it in a large bowl.

Push it away with your hands, like this.

The dough will become smooth and stretchy.

2. Add the poppy seeds and a tablespoon of sesame seeds. Begin to make the dough, following the instructions on the package.

3. The instructions will tell you to 'knead' the dough. Put the dough on a floured work surface, then push the dough away from you.

4. Fold the dough in half, turn it and push it away again. Do this for about five minutes. Leave the dough in a bowl to rise for the time it says on the package.

Cover the rest of the dough in foodwrap while you are rolling each stick.

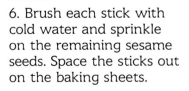

5. Turn on your oven. Cut the dough in quarters, then cut each quarter into five pieces. Roll each piece into an 8in. stick.

6. Brush each stick with cold water and sprinkle on the remaining sesame seeds. Space the sticks out on the baking sheets.

7. Cook the breadsticks for 15 minutes, until they turn golden. Use a spatula and fork to lift them onto a wire rack to cool.

Bread and cheese pudding

Enough for 4

margarine for greasing
6oz. stale white bread (about 6 slices)
4oz. Cheddar cheese
3 eggs
1¾ cups milk
½ teaspoon of spicy brown mustard

salt and ground black pepper
½ teaspoon of ground paprika
2 medium tomatoes

a shallow 1-quart ovenproof dish

Heat your oven to 400°F.

1. Dip a paper towel into some margarine. Rub the paper towel over the inside of an ovenproof dish, to grease it.

2. If the bread is unsliced, slice it. Cut the slices into squares, about 1in., leaving the crust on. Put the bread into the dish.

3. Cut the cheese into ½in. cubes, then scatter them evenly over the bread. Turn your oven on to heat up.

4. Break the eggs into a cup and beat them with a fork. Add the milk, mustard and a little salt and pepper, and whisk it.

5. Slowly pour the milky mixture over the bread and cheese. Make sure that all the pieces are coated with the mixture.

6. Leave the dish to stand for five minutes, so that the egg and milk is absorbed into the bread and it becomes slightly soggy.

7. Sprinkle small pinches of paprika over the top. Wash your hands after touching it because it will sting if you accidentally rub your eyes.

Use a serrated knife.

8. Cut the tomatoes in half and slice them as thinly as you can. Lay the slices in rows on top of the bread and cheese.

9. Put the dish into the oven and bake it for 35 minutes, until the bread is golden brown and the cheese is bubbling.

Tropical spiced rice

Enough for 4

⅓ cup shredded coconut
8oz. can of pineapple pieces in juice
¼ teaspoon of ground tumeric
salt and ground white pepper
8oz. (1⅓ cups) basmati and wild rice, or long-grain
    and wild rice
8 green onions
1 tablespoon of sunflower oil
¼ teaspoon of ground coriander
½ cup frozen peas, thawed
¼ cup raisins

1. Put some water on to boil. Put the shredded coconut into a measuring cup.

2. Pour 2¾ cups of boiling water into the cup. Stir the mixture well.

You could use long grain rice for this recipe. Follow the cooking instructions on its package.

3. Drain the pieces of pineapple through a strainer into a large cup or bowl. Don't throw away the pineapple juice.

4. Pour the coconut liquid and the pineapple juice into a large pan. Add the tumeric and half a teaspoon of salt. Bring it to a boil.

5. Put the rice into a strainer and rinse it well under cold water. Add the rice to the pan and bring it back to a boil.

Don't lift the lid while it cooks.

6. Turn the heat down so that the water is just bubbling. Put a lid on the pan. Cook the rice gently for 20 minutes.

7. While the rice is cooking, cut the top and bottom off the green onions. Slice the onions into 1in. pieces.

8. Heat the oil in a frying pan over medium heat. Add the onions and cook them for four minutes, stirring occasionally.

Cooking rice

Stir it all the time.

9. Sprinkle the coriander over the onions and cook for one minute, stirring all the time. Then, turn the heat off under this pan.

10. When the rice is cooked, add the pineapple, peas, onions, raisins and some pepper. Cook it for a minute, then eat it while it's hot.

If rice sticks together when it is cooked, separate the grains by stirring lightly with a fork.

Italian bread

Enough for 4

2 cups all-purpose flour
1 level teaspoon of easy-blend
   dried yeast
1 cup warm water

flour for work surface
margarine for greasing
6 tablespoons of olive oil
1 teaspoon of sea salt (optional)

a baking sheet, greased with margarine

1. Shake the flour through a strainer into a large bowl. Stir in the easy-blend yeast, then make a hollow in the middle of the flour.

2. Pour the warm water into the hollow, along with five tablespoons of oil. Mix it into the flour with a wooden spoon.

3. Continue mixing the flour, oil and water until you get a soft dough which doesn't stick to the sides of the bowl.

Sprinkle about two tablespoons of flour on your work surface.

4. Sprinkle flour onto a clean, dry work surface. Dip a paper towel in margarine and grease inside a large bowl.

5. Wash your hands. 'Knead' the dough for five minutes (see steps 3 and 4 on page 7), then put it into the greased bowl.

6. Cover the bowl with plastic foodwrap. Leave it in a warm place for an hour, until the dough rises to twice its size.

Remember to grease the baking sheet first.

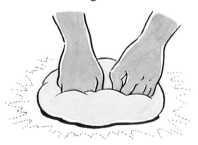

7. Then, knead the dough again for a couple of minutes, to burst all the large air bubbles which have formed inside it.

8. Sprinkle some flour onto a rolling pin, then roll out the dough to make a circle about 10in. across the middle.

9. Put the dough on a baking sheet. Rub oil onto a piece of foodwrap and cover the bread. Turn your oven on to 425°F.

Dip your finger in flour before you press it in.

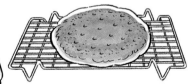

10. Leave the baking sheet in a warm place (not in the oven!) for 20 minutes. Take off the foodwrap. Make dimples all over the top.

11. Brush the top with a tablespoon of oil, then sprinkle the sea salt over the top. Put the baking sheet into the oven.

12. Bake the bread for 25 minutes, until it is golden. Leave it on a wire rack to cool. Cut it into wedges, then add a filling you like.

Mexican bean soup

Enough for 4

1 small red onion
1 clove of garlic
1 tablespoon of olive oil
7oz. can of red kidney beans
1 teaspoon of mild chili powder
14½oz. can of chopped
tomatoes with herbs
1 vegetable bouillon cube

1. Peel the skin off the onion and chop the onion finely. Peel the clove of garlic and crush it. Put some water on to boil.

2. Heat the oil in a large saucepan over medium heat. Cook the onion and garlic for about five minutes until they are soft.

3. Open the can of beans, then pour them into a strainer to drain them. Rinse the beans under cold running water.

Stir until the bouillon cube dissolves.

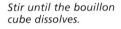

4. Add the beans to the pan, along with the chili powder and chopped tomatoes. Stir everything together well.

5. Crumble the bouillon cube into a measuring cup. Pour in ⅔ cup of boiling water and stir well. Pour the bouillon into the pan.

6. Turn up the heat so that the mixture boils. Then, when it is boiling, turn the heat down so that the soup bubbles gently.

Softening onions

7. Put a lid on the pan and let the soup bubble for about ten minutes. Stir it occasionally to stop it from sticking.

8. Take the pan off the heat. Ladle the soup into bowls. Don't try to pour it out as it may splash. Eat it while it's hot.

When you soften onions, let them sizzle gently in oil, stirring occasionally. Turn the heat down if the onion begins to turn brown.

Bulghur wheat risotto

Enough for 4

4 green onions
4oz. button mushrooms
3 tablespoons of sunflower oil
2oz. flaked almonds
1 vegetable bouillon cube
8oz. bulghur wheat
8 ready-to-eat dried apricots
4 sprigs of fresh parsley
salt and ground black pepper

Stir the almonds all the time, as they burn easily.

1. Cut the tops and bottoms off the green onions. Cut the onions diagonally into pieces, about 1in. long.

2. Wipe the mushrooms with a damp paper towel to clean them. Then, slice each mushroom thinly. Put some water on to boil.

3. Put about half a tablespoon of oil into a saucepan, over medium heat. Cook the almonds until they are golden.

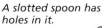
A slotted spoon has holes in it.

Stir until the cube dissolves.

4. Put a paper towel onto a plate. Use a slotted spoon to lift the almonds onto it. Then, heat the remaining oil in the pan.

5. Add the mushrooms and green onions to the pan. Cook them gently for five minutes, until they are soft. Stir them often.

6. Meanwhile, crumble the bouillon cube into a measuring cup. Pour in two cups of boiling water and stir.

Take off the lid and stir it occasionally.

7. Add the bulghur wheat to the pan and stir it for a minute. Pour in the bouillon, then turn the heat up so that the mixture boils.

8. Once it has boiled, turn the heat down and put a lid on the pan. Let the mixture bubble gently for about ten minutes.

9. Use kitchen scissors to snip the apricots into small pieces. Add the pieces to the bubbling mixture, along with some salt and pepper.

Use kitchen scissors.

10. Take the lid off the pan. Let the mixture cook for five minutes more, or until all the bouillon has been absorbed.

11. While the mixture is cooking, break the stalks off the parsley. Put the leaves into a mug and snip them into small pieces.

12. Stir the parsley and half of the flaked almonds into the mixture. Sprinkle the rest of the almonds on top and serve immediately.

Super spaghetti sauce

Enough for 4

1 onion
1 stick of celery
4oz. button mushrooms
2 medium carrots
1 clove of garlic
3 tablespoons of olive oil
1 vegetable bouillon cube

14oz. can of chopped tomatoes
1 tablespoon of Italian seasoning
4oz. meatless burger mix
salt and ground black pepper
12oz. dried pasta or 15oz. fresh pasta
1 tablespoon margarine

1. Cut the ends off the onion and celery. Peel the onion and wash the celery. Cut both the onion and celery into thin slices.

2. Wipe the mushrooms with a damp paper towel. Cut them into thick slices. Peel or scrape the carrots, then slice them finely.

3. Peel and crush the garlic. Heat two tablespoons of oil in a large pan over a low heat. Add the onion and cook it for three minutes.

4. Add the celery, carrots, mushrooms and garlic. Cook them for five minutes, until the onion begins to turn brown.

5. While the vegetables are cooking, put some water on to boil. Crumble the bouillon cube into a measuring cup.

6. Pour two cups of boiling water into the measuring cup and stir until the bouillon cube dissolves.

Stir it occasionally to stop it from sticking.

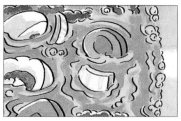

7. Pour the bouillon into the pan. Add the chopped tomatoes, Italian seasoning and a little salt and pepper. Stir the mixture well.

8. Stir in the burger mix. Turn up the heat and bring the mixture to a boil. Then, turn down the heat so that it bubbles gently.

9. Put a lid on the pan and cook the mixture for 30 minutes. The mixture will thicken as the burger soaks up the bouillon.

The oil will stop the pasta from sticking.

Drain the pasta in a colander.

10. About 15 minutes before the sauce is ready, half-fill a large pan with water. Add a tablespoon of oil and a pinch of salt.

11. Bring the water to a boil and add the pasta. Look at the instructions on the package of pasta and cook it for the time it says.

12. When the pasta is cooked, drain it, then put it back into the pan. Add the margarine and shake the pan to coat the pasta.

13. Put the pasta onto four plates or bowls. Ladle some sauce on top and eat it immediately.

Cheese and tomato tart

Enough for 4-6

13oz. package of ready-rolled puff pastry
1 tablespoon of milk
1 large onion
1 medium zucchini
3 tablespoons of olive oil
half a teaspoon of dried oregano
salt and ground black pepper
8oz. cherry tomatoes
8oz. mozzarella cheese

Trim the pastry to fit the tray.

1. Turn your oven on to 425°F. Unroll the pastry. Put it on a baking sheet. Trim one end off, if you need to.

2. Put the milk into a cup. Use a pastry brush to brush the milk around the edge of the pastry, to make a ½ in. border.

3. Cut the ends off the onion and peel it. Cut it finely. Cut the ends off the zucchini and cut it into ½ in. slices.

The onion and zucchini will soften.

4. Heat the oil over lowish heat and add the onion. Cook it for five minutes. Add the zucchini and cook for five minutes more.

5. Stir in the oregano and add some salt and pepper. Spoon the mixture over the pastry, but do not cover the milky border.

6. Use a serrated knife to cut the tomatoes in half. Arrange the tomatoes on top of the mixture, with their cut-side upward.

This tart is delicious served hot or warm.

7. Open the bag of cheese and pour away any liquid. Cut the cheese into ½ in. cubes. Scatter them evenly over the tomatoes.

8. Put the tart on the middle shelf of the oven for 35-40 minutes, until the pastry rises around the edges and turns brown.

9. Leave the tart on the baking sheet for three minutes. Cut the tart into eight pieces. Use a spatula to lift each piece.

Veggie burgers

Makes 8

1 onion
1 stick of celery
1 red pepper
2 tablespoons of sunflower oil
1 clove of garlic
6oz. dried red lentils
1 vegetable bouillon cube
half a teaspoon of yeast extract
3oz. fresh breadcrumbs (approx. 3 slices)
2oz. chopped nuts
ground black pepper

Stir it occasionally.

1. Cut the ends off the onion and celery. Peel the onion and wash the celery. Cut them both into very thin pieces.

2. Slice the ends off the red pepper. Cut it in half and cut out the seeds. Cut each half into thin strips. Cut the strips into cubes.

3. Put some water on to boil. Heat the oil in a pan over medium heat. Cook the onion and celery for five minutes, until soft.

Stir it all the time, to coat everything with oil.

4. Peel and crush the garlic. Add it to the pan, along with the red pepper and lentils. Cook them for about a minute.

5. Crumble the bouillon cube into a measuring cup and pour in 1½ cups of boiling water. Add the yeast extract and stir well.

6. Pour the bouillon into the pan and bring it to a boil. Then, turn the heat down until the mixture bubbles gently. Put a lid on the pan.

Cover it with plastic foodwrap.

7. Cook the mixture for 25 minutes, or until the lentils have absorbed all the bouillon. Spoon the mixture into a large bowl.

8. Mix in the breadcrumbs, nuts and some pepper. Let the mixture cool, then cover it. Put it in a refrigerator for at least 30 minutes.

9. When chilled, divide the mixture into eight pieces. Sprinkle some flour on a chopping board and roll each piece into a ball.

Use a spatula to turn the burgers over.

10. Turn your broiler on to medium. Press each ball into a burger shape and brush the top of each one with a little oil.

11. Put the burgers onto the broiler-pan rack. Cook them under the broiler for five minutes, until they are slightly browned.

12. Turn the burgers over. Brush the tops with a little more oil and cook them for five more minutes. Eat them while they are hot.

Mushroom croustade

Enough for 4

For the case:
½ cup whole-wheat flour
¼ cup oatmeal
1 cup breadcrumbs (find out how to make breadcrumbs on page 4)
½ cup butter or margarine

For the filling:
8oz. button mushrooms
1 tablespoon of sunflower oil
2 eggs
5oz. vegetarian cream-style cheese with herbs and garlic
salt and ground black pepper

an 8 inch quiche dish

Mix them with a wooden spoon.

1. Turn your oven on to 400°F. to heat up. For the case, put the flour, oatmeal and breadcrumbs into a large bowl.

2. Gently melt the butter or margarine in a pan over low heat. Pour in the mixture from the bowl and mix it well.

3. Spoon the mixture into a quiche dish. Use the back of a spoon to press it firmly onto the bottom and up the sides of the dish.

The baking sheet helps the mixture to cook on the bottom.

Stir the mushrooms occasionally.

4. Put the dish onto a baking sheet. Bake it on the middle shelf of your oven for ten minutes. Take it out of the oven.

5. Turn the oven down to 350°F. Wipe the mushrooms using a damp paper towel, then cut them in half.

6. Heat the oil in a frying pan over low heat. Add the mushrooms and cook them for five minutes, until they are soft.

Put the bowl on a damp cloth to stop it from slipping.

Use a wooden spoon.

7. Turn the heat off under the mushrooms. Break the eggs into a small bowl and beat them with a fork until they are mixed.

8. Put the cheese into a bowl and stir it. Add the beaten egg, a little at a time. Stir the mixture each time you add some egg.

9. Add the mushrooms to the mixture, but don't add any of the juice left in the pan. Add some salt and pepper and stir well.

The croustade is delicious served with a salad or green vegetables.

10. Spoon the mixture into the dish and smooth the top with the back of a spoon. Press in any mushrooms sticking up.

11. Put the dish into the oven for 25 minutes and bake it until the filling has set and the crust is golden. Serve it hot or cold.

Cheesy sausages

Makes 8

1 small leek
1 tablespoon butter
4oz. Cheddar cheese
8 fresh chives
2 eggs
salt and ground black pepper
$\frac{1}{4}$ teaspoon of mustard powder
$1\frac{1}{2}$ cups (6oz.) white breadcrumbs
2 tablespoons of all-purpose flour
2 tablespoons of sunflower oil

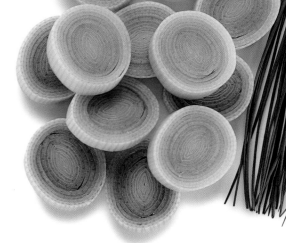

Slice halfway along the leek from the green end, like this.

Use a small saucepan.

Snip the chives over the bowl.

1. Cut the roots and green tops off the leek. Make a slice halfway along the leek and rinse it really well to get rid of any soil. Then, slice the leek finely.

2. Melt the butter in a saucepan over medium heat. Add the slices of leek and cook gently for about five minutes, until soft. Don't let them go brown.

3. Spoon the leek into a big bowl. Grate the cheese finely and add it to the bowl. Use kitchen scissors to snip the chives into small pieces and add them too.

Put a damp dishcloth under the bowl to stop it from slipping as you beat.

Find out how to make breadcrumbs on page 4.

4. Break the eggs into a small bowl. Add some salt and pepper and the mustard. Beat them lightly until the yolks, egg white and mustard are mixed.

5. Pour the beaten egg mixture into the big bowl and add the breadcrumbs. Stir everything together with a wooden spoon until it is mixed well.

6. Sprinkle a little flour onto a clean, dry work surface. Put the mixture onto the flour and cut it into eight equal pieces with a knife.

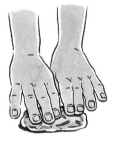

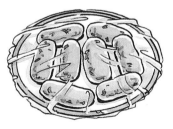

Turn the sausages often as they cook.

7. Wash your hands and dry them. Rub a little flour on your hands, then roll each piece into the shape of a sausage. Put the sausages onto a plate.

8. Cover the sausages with some plastic foodwrap. Put the plate into a refrigerator for about 20 minutes, to make the sausages firm.

9. When the sausages are ready, heat the oil in a frying pan over medium heat. Add the sausages and cook them for ten minutes. Serve immediately.

Chunky goulash

Enough for 4

1 onion
1 clove of garlic
2 carrots
2 medium-sized potatoes

half a head of cauliflower
1 tablespoon of vegetable oil
3 teaspoons of paprika
1 tablespoon of flour
1 vegetable bouillon cube
14½ oz. can of chopped tomatoes
with herbs
salt and ground black pepper
⅔ cup sour cream

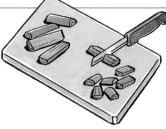

1. Cut the top and bottom off the onion. Peel the onion and cut it into small chunks. Peel the clove of garlic and crush it.

2. Peel or scrape the carrots and cut them in half. Cut them lengthwise, then slice them into pieces about an inch long.

3. Peel the potatoes and cut them in half. Cut each piece of potato into ½ in. slices, then cut the slices into cubes.

4. Pull any leaves off the cauliflower and throw them away. Cut the florets off the cauliflower's stalk (see tip below).

5. Heat the oil in a large pan over lowish heat. Gently cook the onion and garlic for five minutes, until they are soft.

6. While the onions are cooking, put some water on to boil. Sprinkle 2 teaspoons of paprika over the onions. Add the flour and stir well.'

7. Crumble the bouillon cube into a measuring cup and pour in 2¾ cups of boiling water. Stir it until the cube dissolves.

8. Pour the bouillon into the pan. Add the tomatoes, carrots, potatoes and the cauliflower florets, as well as a little salt and pepper.

9. Turn the heat up and bring the mixture to a boil. Then, turn down the heat so that the mixture bubbles gently.

Cutting cauliflower

10. Put a lid on the pan. Leave everything to bubble gently for about 20-25 minutes, until the vegetables are cooked.

11. Use a ladle to put the goulash into bowls. Spoon on some sour cream and sprinkle the remaining paprika on top.

Cut into the stalk about ½ in. from a floret. Pull the floret out, then cut off another one.

Baked Spanish omelette

Enough for 4

margarine for greasing
1 onion
2 medium potatoes
2 tablespoons of olive oil
1 clove of garlic
¾ cup frozen peas, thawed
4 eggs
⅔ cup milk
salt and ground black pepper

a shallow 8-inch ovenproof dish

1. Turn your oven on to 350°F. Dip a paper towel in some margarine, then rub it over the inside of the dish.

2. Peel the onion and cut it finely. Peel the potatoes and cut them in half. Cut them into ½in. slices. Cut the slices into cubes.

Stir it occasionally.

3. Heat the oil in a frying pan over medium heat. Add the onion and potato and cook for four minutes, until they begin to soften.

Stir it all the time.

4. Peel and crush the garlic. Add it to the pan and cook for two minutes more, until the onion and potatoes begin to brown.

5. Take the pan off the heat. Spoon the onion and potato into the bottom of the dish spreading it out evenly. Add the peas too.

6. Break the eggs into a small bowl. Beat them with a fork, then stir in the milk and a little salt and black pepper.

7. Pour the beaten egg over the vegetables in the dish. Bake the omelette in the oven for 45 minutes until it has set.

8. To check that it is cooked, push a knife into the middle of it. If lots of liquid seeps out, cook it for a few more minutes.

9. Run a knife around the edge of the dish to loosen the omelette, then cut it into quarters. Use a spatula to serve it.

Other fillings : Cheese

Sprinkle 2oz. of grated Swiss cheese and one tablespoon of chopped parsley over the vegetables, at step 5.

Mushroom

For a mushroom omelette, leave out the peas. Slice 4oz. of mushrooms. Cook them with the onions and potatoes at step 3.

Tomato

Slice two medium-sized tomatoes as finely as you can. Arrange the slices on top of the cooked vegetables, at step 5.

Corn

Drain a 7oz. can of corn in a strainer or colander. Sprinkle the corn over the vegetables at step 5.

Cheese bites with tomato sauce

Enough for 4

For the tomato sauce:
1 red onion
1 tablespoon of olive oil
14oz. can of chopped tomatoes
2 tablespoons of soy sauce
2 teaspoons of red wine vinegar
1 teaspoon of soft brown sugar

For the cheese bites:
3oz. (¾ cup) white breadcrumbs
2 tablespoons of plain flour
8oz. Cheddar cheese
salt and ground black pepper
2 eggs (you only need the whites)
oil for frying

Grate the cheese on the medium holes on your grater.

Slice the onion as thinly as you can.

1. Make the breadcrumbs (see page 4). Put ½ cup (2oz.) of the breadcrumbs into a bowl. Grate the cheese, add it and stir well.

2. Put the bowl on one side while you make the sauce. Cut the ends off the onion and peel it. Cut it in half, then slice it.

3. Put the olive oil into a pan over a low heat. Cook the slices of onion for five minutes, stirring them occasionally.

4. Add the tomatoes, soy sauce, vinegar and sugar and stir it well. Turn up the heat and bring the mixture to a boil.

5. Once the mixture has boiled, turn down the heat and let it bubble gently. Put a lid on the pan and cook for 15 minutes.

6. Make the bites while the sauce is cooking. Shake the flour and some salt and pepper through a strainer onto the cheese.

Make sure that the bowl is clean before you start.

You don't need the yolks.

7. Carefully break one egg onto a saucer. Put an egg cup over the yolk. Tip the saucer over a bowl so that the white dribbles into it.

8. Do the same with the other egg. Whisk the egg white until it is stiff and makes points or 'peaks' when you lift your whisk.

9. If the tomato sauce is ready while you are still cooking the bites, turn down the heat under it, as low as it will go.

10. Stir a large spoonful of the egg white into the cheese and breadcrumb mixture. Then, gently stir in the rest of the white.

11. Wash your hands. Put the remaining breadcrumbs onto a plate. Make 16 balls with the mixture, about the size of ping pong balls.

12. Roll the balls in the crumbs to coat them. Pour about ½in. of oil into a frying pan. Turn the heat on to medium.

Use a spatula to lift them into the pan.

13. After a minute or so, put eight balls into the pan. Cook them for five minutes. Turn the balls as they cook so they are golden all over.

14. Use a slotted spoon to lift them out. Put them onto some paper towels to drain. Cook the rest of the balls in the same way.

15. Put four balls onto each plate. Stir the tomato sauce, then spoon it over the balls. Eat them while they are hot.

You could put some sauce onto each plate before you add the bites. Spoon any remaining sauce on top.

Tofu skewers with noodles

Enough for 4

20oz. package of firm tofu
2 tablespoons of soy sauce
1 small onion
1 clove of garlic
2 tablespoons of sunflower oil
¼ cup shredded coconut
1 tablespoon of lemon or lime juice

1 tablespoon of soft brown sugar
¼ teaspoon of chili powder
2 tablespoons of crunchy peanut butter

For the noodles:
1 tablespoon of oil
8oz. dried or 12oz. fresh egg noodles
1 vegetable bouillon cube
2 tablespoons of chopped parsley
  or coriander

eight skewers or kebab sticks
    (If you use wooden sticks, soak
        them in water for ten minutes
        before you begin.)

Use medium heat.

1. Open the package of tofu and drain off any liquid. Pat the tofu dry on a paper towel, then cut it into one inch cubes.

2. Push the cubes onto the sticks. Put a tablespoon of soy sauce into a bowl and brush it all over the cubes. Put some water on to boil.

3. Peel the onion and cut it finely. Peel and crush the garlic. Heat the oil in a saucepan and cook the onion and garlic until soft.

Stir until the coconut dissolves.

4. Put the shredded coconut in a bowl. Pour in three tablespoons of boiling water and stir.

5. Add the lemon or lime juice, the brown sugar, chili powder, peanut butter and a tablespoon of soy sauce.

6. Stir everything together until it is blended, then mix in the onion and garlic. Brush the mixture over the tofu.

The oil stops the noodles from sticking together.

Watch the tofu, it can burn easily.

7. Half-fill a large saucepan with water and bring it to a boil. Crumble the bouillon cube and stir it in. Add a tablespoon of oil.

8. Turn the broiler on to medium. Put the tofu sticks onto the rack in the broiler pan and put the pan under the broiler.

9. Cook the tofu for eight minutes in total. Every two minutes, turn the sticks and brush the tofu with more peanut mixture.

Time the cooking from when the noodles began to boil.

10. Meanwhile, add the noodles to the water. Let the water boil again, then turn down the heat so the water bubbles gently.

11. Cook the noodles for the time it says on their package then drain them. Put them back into the pan. Add the parsley or coriander.

12. Toss the noodles in the parsley or coriander. Put the noodles onto plates and lay two tofu sticks on top. Eat while hot.

Eggs flamenco

Enough for 4

1 medium onion
1 small red pepper
1 small yellow pepper
1 clove of garlic
1 zucchini
2 tablespoons of olive oil

14½oz. can of chopped tomatoes
1 teaspoon of bouquet garni
salt and ground black pepper
butter or margarine for greasing
4 eggs

a shallow, ovenproof dish

1. Turn on your oven to 375°F. Cut the ends off the onion and peel it. Slice the onion as finely as you can.

2. Slice the ends off the peppers and cut them in half. Cut out the seeds. Cut the peppers into strips, then into cubes.

3. Peel the clove of garlic and crush it in a garlic press. Cut the ends off the zucchini and cut it into thin slices.

Stir the mixture occasionally.

4. Heat the oil in a pan over medium heat. Add the onions, garlic, peppers and zucchini. Cook them for ten minutes.

5. When the vegetables are soft, add the tomatoes, herbs and a pinch of salt and pepper. Stir it and let the mixture bubble.

6. Leave the mixture to cook for about five minutes, or until the sauce becomes thicker and the amount has reduced a little.

7. While the mixture is cooking, dip a paper towel into some margarine or butter. Rub it over an ovenproof dish to grease it.

Space the hollows evenly.

8. When the mixture is ready, spoon it into the dish. Use the back of the spoon to make four hollows in the mixture.

9. Carefully crack an egg into each hollow. Lift the dish into the oven, without letting the eggs spill out over the mixture.

Breaking eggs

Bake the mixture until the egg whites have set.

10. Cook the eggs for about 10-15 minutes if you like runny yolks, or 15-20 minutes if you like your eggs well-cooked.

To break an egg, tap it sharply on the side of a bowl or a cup. Tap it again, but harder, if the shell doesn't crack the first time.

Push your thumbs inside the crack and pull the shell apart gently. Try not to let any pieces of shell fall into the bowl or cup.

Vegetarian sausages in batter

Enough for 4

12oz. package of vegetarian sausages,
  thawed if frozen
1 medium zucchini
6 cherry tomatoes
½ cup flour

¼ teaspoon of salt
¼ cup milk
1 egg
2 tablespoons solid white vegetable
  shortening

a 8-inch round pan

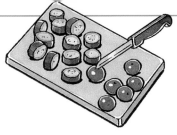

Use a
large bowl.

1. Turn your oven on to 425°F. to heat up. Cut each sausage into three equal-sized pieces.

2. Cut the ends off the zucchini. Cut it into one inch slices. Prick the skin of each tomato with the tip of a sharp knife.

3. To make the batter, shake the flour and salt through a strainer. Then, make a hollow in the middle of the flour.

4. Pour the milk into a measuring cup and add ¼ cup of cold water to make ½ cup of liquid altogether.

5. Break the egg into a cup, then pour it into the hollow in the flour. Pour in half of the milky liquid from the cup, too.

Whisk it until you get a smooth batter.

6. Mix the milky liquid with the flour. Add the rest of the liquid, a little at a time. Whisk it well each time you add some.

7. Put the fat into the pan and put it in the oven for five minutes. Then, wearing oven mitts, very carefully lift the pan out.

8. Spread the sausages and vegetables around the pan. Be careful, the fat will be hot. Then, pour the batter over them.

9. Bake it on the top shelf of the oven for 30-35 minutes, until it has risen and has turned golden. Cut into four and serve.

Tortillas with black bean filling

Enough for 4

margarine or oil for greasing
1 small onion
1 clove of garlic
1 tablespoon of olive oil
two 14½oz. cans of black beans or
  pinto beans
two 14½oz. cans of chopped tomatoes
  with basil
1 tablespoon of tomato purée

2 tablespoons of dried cilantro
1 tablespoon of mild chili powder
salt and ground black pepper
10oz. Cheddar cheese
8 ready-made flour tortillas
½ cup sour cream or plain yogurt

a large shallow, ovenproof dish, about
  14 x 8in.

Heat your oven 400°F.

1. Dip a paper towel into some margarine or pour a little oil onto it. Rub the paper towel inside the dish, to grease it.

2. Turn your oven on. Cut the ends off the onion and peel it, then slice it finely. Peel the clove of garlic and crush it.

3. Heat the oil in a saucepan. Cook the onion and the garlic over medium heat for five minutes, until soft.

Drain the beans in a strainer or a colander.

4. Drain the beans. Rinse them under cold running water. Add them to the pan and cook for a minute, stirring all the time.

5. Stir in the chopped tomatoes, tomato purée, cilantro and chili powder. Add a little salt and pepper, too.

6. Turn up the heat and bring the sauce to a boil. Then, turn the heat down so that the sauce is still bubbling, but more gently.

7. Let the sauce cook for 20 minutes, stirring now and then to stop it from sticking. The sauce should begin to thicken.

The sauce should be thick enough to sit on the spoon.

8. If your sauce doesn't start to thicken, turn the heat up a little until the mixture bubbles more. Stir it often.

9. While the sauce is cooking, grate the cheese on the large holes on the grater. Lay the tortillas on a clean, dry work surface.

Be careful as you roll them. The sauce is still hot.

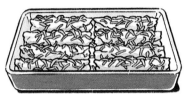

10. Divide the sauce between the tortillas. Spread it out almost to the edges, with the back of a spoon.

11. Sprinkle half of the cheese over the tortillas, then roll them up. Then, lay them, seam-side down, in the dish.

12. Sprinkle the rest of the cheese over the tortillas. Bake them for 15 minutes, then serve them with the sour cream or yogurt.

Stuffed peppers

Enough for 4

4 medium peppers
4 tablespoons of olive oil
1 vegetable bouillon cube
6oz. (1 cup) long-grain rice
1 small red onion
1 clove of garlic
7oz. can of chopped tomatoes
half a teaspoon of dried bouquet garni
½ cup frozen peas, thawed
salt and ground black pepper

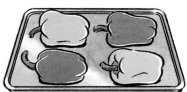

1. Turn your oven on to 400°F. Wash and dry the peppers, then put them onto a baking sheet.

2. Put two tablespoons of oil in a cup. Brush it over the peppers. Put the sheet into the oven and bake the peppers for 12 minutes.

3. When the peppers are cooked, leave them until they are cool enough to touch. Cut them in half from top to bottom.

Pour the bouillon into a large pan.

4. Cut the stalk, core and seeds from each pepper. Pat the peppers dry, then put them back onto the sheet. Put some water on to boil.

5. Crumble the bouillon cube into a cup. Pour 2¾ cups of boiling water into the cup. Stir well and pour the bouillon into a pan.

6. Add another 2¾ cups of boiling water. Pour in the rice and stir well. Turn the heat down so the mixture bubbles gently.

7. Leave the rice to cook for about ten minutes until it is just tender, then drain it in a large strainer over a sink.

8. While the rice is cooking, cut the ends off the onion and peel it. Slice the onion as finely as you can. Peel and crush the garlic.

9. Heat two tablespoons of oil in a pan. Add the onion and garlic, and cook them gently until they are soft.

The oil stops the foil from sticking to the peppers.

10. Stir in the tomatoes, herbs and a little salt and pepper. Leave the mixture to bubble gently for about five minutes.

11. Add the rice and peas to the tomato mixture and mix everything well. Spoon the mixture into the halves of pepper.

12. Spread a little oil onto the dull side of a piece of foil. Cover the peppers. Put them into the oven for ten minutes. Eat while hot.

Spinach strudel

Enough for 4

4oz. pine nuts
6oz. frozen chopped spinach, thawed
9oz. ricotta cheese
quarter of a teaspoon of grated nutmeg
salt and ground black pepper

3 tablespoons butter
4oz. fillo dough (about 8 sheets)
1 tablespoon of poppy seeds
1 tablespoon Italian seasoning

Heat your oven to 400°F.

1. Turn on your oven. Put the pine nuts on a baking sheet. Bake them in the oven for five minutes, until golden. Let them cool.

2. Put the spinach into a strainer. Press the spinach with the back of a large spoon, to squeeze out as much liquid as you can.

3. Put the spinach into a bowl. Mix in the pine nuts, the ricotta cheese, nutmeg, Italian seasoning and a little salt and pepper.

Cover the rest of the dough, (see tip, below right).

Don't forget to brush each sheet with butter before putting another one on top.

4. Put the butter into a small saucepan. Heat it very gently over a low heat until the butter melts. Don't let it burn.

5. Carefully lift one sheet of fillo dough and put it on a clean dish towel. Brush the sheet of dough with some of the melted butter.

6. Put another sheet of fillo dough on top and brush it with butter. Add the other sheets of dough, one by one, in the same way.

Spread out the mixture with a spatula.

Roll it like a Swiss roll.

7. Spoon the spinach mixture onto the dough. Spread it over the dough, leaving a one inch border around the edge.

8. Fold each of the short sides of dough over carefully, so that they overlap the edge of the spinach mixture.

9. Fold one of the long sides of dough over onto the mixture. Then, roll it over and over until you reach the other long side.

10. Brush some of the melted butter over a baking sheet to grease it. Lift the strudel onto it, seam-side down.

11. Brush the top and sides of the strudel with the rest of the melted butter. Sprinkle poppy seeds all over the top.

12. Bake the strudel in the oven for 20 minutes, until it is golden and crisp. Cut it into slices and eat it right away.

Using fillo dough

To stop fillo dough from drying out, cover the sheets of dough with a clean, damp dish towel until you need to use them.

Nut crumble

Enough for 4

1 carrot and 1 parsnip
8oz. broccoli
8oz. turnips
8oz. sweet potato
salt and ground black pepper
1 onion
3 tablespoons butter
⅓ cup plain flour
2 cups milk

1 teaspoon dried bouquet garni
margarine for greasing

For the crumble:
1 cup flour
⅓ cup butter
⅓ cup oatmeal
2oz. chopped mixed nuts

a large ovenproof dish

1. Turn your oven on to 375°F. Peel the carrot and the parsnip. Cut them into 1in. pieces.

2. Cut the florets off the broccoli stalks. Peel the turnip and sweet potato and cut them in half. Cut each half into 1in. slices.

3. Cut the slices of turnip and sweet potato into cubes. Half-fill a large saucepan with water and add half a teaspoon of salt.

4. Bring the pan of water to a boil. Add the carrot, parsnip, turnip and sweet potato and bring the water back to a boil.

5. Turn down the heat so that the water bubbles gently, then put a lid on the pan. Leave it to cook for five minutes.

6. Add the broccoli and cook it for five minutes more. Ladle ⅔ cup of the cooking water into a cup. Drain away the rest.

Stir the onion occasionally.

7. To make the sauce, cut the ends off the onion, peel it and slice it. Melt the butter over low heat. Cook the onion for five minutes.

8. Stir in the flour and cook it for one minute. Take the pan off the heat and add a little of the milk. Stir it really well.

9. Continue stirring in the milk, a little at a time. Stir in the water you saved from cooking the vegetables and the bouquet garni.

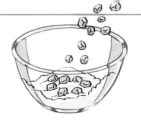

10. Put the pan back onto the heat. Bring the sauce to a boil slowly, stirring all the time. Let the sauce boil for one minute.

11. Grease the dish with margarine. Spoon in the vegetables and sprinkle on some pepper. Pour the sauce over the vegetables.

12. To make the crumble, shake the flour through a strainer into a large bowl. Cut the butter into small chunks. Add it to the bowl.

13. Rub the butter into the flour with your fingertips. Lift it up and let it fall as you do it. Continue until it looks like breadcrumbs.

14. Stir in the oatmeal and nuts. Use a spoon to sprinkle the crumble evenly over the vegetables to cover them.

15. Bake the crumble in the oven for 35 minutes. The topping will turn golden brown. Spoon it onto plates and eat while it's hot.

Index

With thanks to Tom and Jeanne Gilbert for help with the American edition.